# A Heavenly Symposium

*poems by*

# Claire-Elise A. Baalke

*Finishing Line Press*
Georgetown, Kentucky

# A Heavenly Symposium

## ACKNOWLEDGMENTS

I would like to thank my father for his support. If not for him, I would not
have submitted this collection. I would also like to thank my partner, Tyler,
for his constant support of all the things I do and write no matter if they
make sense to him or not. I would like to acknowledge my friend, Tiffany,
whose poetry had inspired some of the work within these pages. Thank
you to all my friends and family who read my writing or don't, but who
encourage me all the same!

Publisher: Leah Huete de Maines
Editor: Christen Kincaid
Cover Art: Hannah Witherington
Author Photo: Sara G. Flores
Cover Design: Elizabeth Maines McCleavy

Order online: www.finishinglinepress.com
also available on amazon.com

Author inquiries and mail orders:
Finishing Line Press
PO Box 1626
Georgetown, Kentucky 40324
USA

# Contents

# PART I:

## Theory & Inspiration

## A Theory of Relativity

I don't remember if the sky looks so large anywhere else
or if the world feels so constricting or my life so small
in other places. What is the force that tethers me
other than my own resolve, as I lie here staring up at the clouds
and they roll over me, inciting an awe—an ancient awe:

> *Look at the eyes in the sky that look down upon us.*
> *What do they see but the mere clay and stones wrought*
> *with sinful desire, uncivilized and premediated ends>*
> *these ends meet nowhere but here, in the heavens,*
> > *this celestium, the honorific of which remains*
> > *above us: up above, here, and down below.*

And now we sing to the heavens this song of strife and longing,
as if the endless toil of our existence is only to glance beyond
the white veil before us, but still we hide our faces, conjuring
new stories for ourselves in other lands.

### *Mea sancta patrona astrologiae* or, The Awakener

You sit across the table
vivisected by books and computer screens:
the artwork on the surrounding walls portrays
birds and colors that dissect our personalities—
this separation clear through both space and time—
though moon is said to represent me most clearly,
I still feel far from your haloed enthusiasm.
The ties that bind us tip with the scales of your
posturing and lies down before your small pocked
beauty marks, which I bow before as for a mighty Babylonian King:
please, beg the eagle for my life's reprise.

# PART II:

## The Planets

### Elektor Hyperion
*The Sun*

It was you that day
riding your chariot above:
*Pyröis, Aeos, Aethon,* and *Phlegon's*
fiery hooves pawing the sky.
Panoptically glancing down to witness
your cows' plight—
Odysseus' men on *Thrinacia,* your sacred isle,
slaughtering them.

But the real blaspheme came from Anaxagoras' lips
when he spoke of you as a red-hot ball of metal,
and not: the restrainer of the serpent-god,
the radiant one, bringer of glad tidings to mortal men;
the rays of your aureole crown likened to arrows,
brother to the moon and dawn, the eye of Zeus,
god of all gods.

Oh, *meteora!* What does it mean to be like the sun?
*Hekatos* rays lighting our auroral vision,
or did someone else pull you across our atmosphere
and give me this little light of mine?
You tip the solar system with your mass,
an encompassing nuclear fission,
and yet, as you dirigibily float above
your age tells the tale of our lives.

## A Hermetic Guise
*Mercury in three parts*

I.

Lightly,
you glide
winged afoot to
Aeneas, after lustful
nightfall in Dido's
heterotopic cavern, vows
secretly spun amiss in the
dewy dawn, eyes laden with love.
Caduceus in hand, you set him
aright toward missions of might
laying claim to Rome, not Carthage.

Because duty trumps love in the eyes of the gods
and no humanly guise sets them astray,
though a homely, beautiful nymph may
seduce the will of the god of boundaries
escorting the dead lover to the underworldly
and Ram produces these invisible household gods, two.

But once, you were merely a heap of stones
carrying Morpheus from the valle of sleep
to the realm of man, a messenger
with cockerel and tortoise besides.
And somewhere you slipped
a slight figure between the
sheets of hermeneutics
and became some
thing else.

II.

                              :Perigee     Aphelion:
                    you ride                         apsis rays

               the                                swift-footed

         high of                              "albedo"

      retrograde                           of you

     appearing                      with dorsa
     in                                  ridges—

     constant                            we
     backward                         sight

     motion—                          you
     but,                            in

      the                          setting

      idea                        of day

     is the                      with

     apotheosis                   your

      of optical                moon-like

       illusion               highlands
        attributed             and
         to your           mercuriality
           lively        suspended
            character.    .beyond

III.

This silver is toxic.

There is a "first matter": something foetid and dark. Three girls in white dresses march through the stench of bog, one losing slipper to the mire—they dive, drag, and pull. But, like a game of posy, it is lost. Now, these lesions and sores fester before dispassionate eyes, grief-laden women springing forth in hallucination with fear of release. This leprosy of the mind ails more than the seeker.

There is something to this alchemical symbolism. They dip hands into stagnant water, fingertips to mold the clay— bringing life to divination, profundity to signs. This belief, these wards we paint protect against good and evil—a disabusing form of weakness as we reach out of the dark, dampened caves striving for greater truth, nails clawing the earth, anguish in eyes that wait in the deep silence of time.

This silver is death.

## Sister Planet

*Venus*

When we looked out on the water during the light,
oh, divine lady, mistress of the ages—
it was not yet July, your month of Etruscan celebration.
A Venusian overcast blocked the backward cycle of your sky.
Arachnoids and coronae are depressions of the surroundings, a false
color masks volcanism in your character.

Rising and falling like the water before you,
Hesperus and Phosphorus as one:
we talked little of the cresting of river rapids and
log encased, shaped as sphinx hiding in the deep.

This sandbar we walk on hides many fossils,
the syncretization of gods and goddesses from the times of
Uruk and before: you prefer veneration, a sprig of myrtle—
the white, dove-like flower juxtaposed with the blood
of war and strife—a bushel of roses, vermilion as your sensual spirit.
Once a sprite, you've flown through time on the backs
of those who worship love, beauty, desire—this
naked, marbled body betrays both virtue and fault.

Inadvertently, you forsook your lover to leave
the underworld, Iananna, yet—
loved him later, the one whose mother you petrified
in bark—mireful, incestuous wife.
Now the river runs crimson with his blood,
stabbed by the boar's tusk—vengeance of a forgotten lover—
and sea anemones grow rampant there.

By the ocean, I stare out at the saltwater pearling on the sand
entranced by your magnificence, born of seafoam,
we watch as you spill your grace over Pandora's box,
which men love to embrace. Still your barrenness is clear—
no humanity will ever live here within your disparity
or the heat of your enshrouding love.

## Tellurian

*Earth*

Child of chaos, tell me what I should do.
I sit on the dock with you and I am fed back the words that I once
said to you.
Birther of all living things, this womb, my home—
the soil that blankets me as I sleep, forest canopies acting umbrella
to the rain: the liquid that runs through your veins.

This cornucopia of life sits before me, a moveable feast, enthroned as
a motherly gift, produced by every fiber of your being.
I eat it. I consume you.

Daughter of order, show me what is right.
You gather my memories of you, keeping them captive, storing them
away for a rainy day.
Lover of humanity, honor me with your grace—
seen rising out of the womb of your own skin, breaching through
to air, you hand off the child to Aphrodite for safe-keeping, as you
also do for me.

This is the crest of your love, the other layers lie beneath as
a sacred promise to be with me always.
I love this. I absorb you.

# Trivia

*The Moon*

When is the best time to cut one's hair? You ask.

It is an old wives' tale that the full moon promotes hair growth,
butchery of the body, a form of sacrifice to the gods:
but, do not slay yourself as Artemis would slay a beast,
though Orion may reach for you, do not use your vigilance for harm,
turn your eyes of light to the shores of the Lake Nemi;
watch the water lap at your toes, pebbles
between icy feet, reverberating forces from the
heavenly bodies—this lunacy knitted together in our brain's
water pulling us from the here and now.

What is this triplicity appearing before me? You question.

These crossroads we travel down in the dark,
we are the primordial instincts: chasing down the soft doe
in the forest beyond, her face is the only light
and after cleansing its flesh and offering the rest to her,
we descend below the surface of the lake
in the crystalline glow of her grace.

## Fire Star

*Mars*

He places green soldiers in the sand before me,
        I place mine, bastioned
by barricade, awaiting the shells and shocks of
            artillery fire;
these devotees of strife—
        discord is their companion.
Terror and fear guard circles around and protect from defeat.
                Father of the people,
you play at judgment of the fate of the dead
        believing in peace through military power
but only love can conquer you, savage beast.
            Now the wolves come to mop up the dead:
a sign of victory,
        but you are caught
as the rooster crows at the light of dawn—
            it is a trap.

## Planetesimals
*The Belt*

I wish to be more like the others,

> but Jupiter holds me back.

I am the star-like dust that fills the void,

> this disability placed upon me by gravitational perturbation—

I cannot become more than I am,

> no matter can I attract—

> no particulates to expand my being as he pulls me in further

> > when he resonates with the Sun,

I discorporate in the gap between, pulled     from body to body

> and thrown out.

My ancient roots mean nothing to the weight of space, or is it time?

## Viniculture

*Jupiter*

Father, you are the one who carries away the spoils,
but my mother always wins at cornhole
whether I'm drunk or not.

These persistent anti-cyclonic storms have existed
since before humans could understand them;
you send the wind and rain to quench the thirst
of these crackling sands leaving dew
to cleanse the seeds as we pour the new wine
into the ditch before your temple,
this building that serves it to us
one small goblet at a time
a waste to sip and spit
liquid unused as these
elves and sprites
snap in the air before us,
within the dusty, gossamer ring of your sacred valley
where culture is grapes and you lord over it—
this jovial beam that holds us together.

# Golden Age
*Saturn*

This is the limit of humanity:
rings of ice and dust surround us
the boundaries of wealth and wheat.
We make haruspex offerings for divination upon
the civilized, ideas passed down from the ancient:
Baal, Satre, Dagon.

This is the melancholic humor:
a veiled sadness, our father of truth
returns now to mark this economic significance—
this mudpuddling for nutrients.
We try to prove our worth,
we are not merely common broad wings
iridescing in the dense woods.

This is the day of freedom some say:
we chose our own merry king to preside
over us in jest, to light these candles of knowledge
that melt the gag wax
I gave them.

This is the great malefic:
a pallid, jaundice age
marking conformity.
This is the time of the sickle.

## The Muse

*Uranus*

It is a weakness, they say, to decay at a slower rate—this
deception creates armor plating, the fissures instability
divides us from one another unlike an extinct swallowtail
moth species "the heavenly one"—broad and unchanging,
only flying in the daylight. But this decay isn't what we think
it is—it existed all along, whether created out of a god's
testicles or Dionian—this colorant, or methane absorption
creates an in-betweenness, an aquamarine or cyan haze,
which similar to the sensation of radiation crawling up
under the skin can easily melt away flesh.

## Equestrus

*Neptune*

Three girls stand a perfect line graph
on either end a brunette, dirty blonde in between
rivaling the frolicking rebellion of half wild horses,
the gelded chosen pretend to be as free—
haltered and barebacked, girls and steeds
enter the man-made stream, running back and forth
across valleyed water, splashing through air and hide.

With Triton raised, he watches from below in watery
depths, he can prevent it here, but not later in
the forest when blonde is thrown from golden,
when the drought and heat penetrate deep
and the mosquitos float heavy in the honey of the summer's breeze.

We are his paredrae, the feminine accompaniment—
salacious and venial, the center holds, balancing between
pouring over and oppressive, yet
quietly flowing—the perfect paradox.

## Dwarfed

*Pluto*

We are easily diminished in the eyes of others,
once a superior prince of the darkness, in transcendence of
matter—spirit over mind—with a great renewal we transform
into a small ice rock, our twin sharing the barycenter.

Our eccentricity dwindles in perception to other
bodies floating out before us with more stable orbital
resonances that keep us tethered here at the edge of the universe,
like the forgotten god of the underworld.

Lord to all who are weak in spirit, the others
do not see our tears of steel falling before Orpheus' melody
of lost love which we understand wholly as
an exploration of the depths of our unconscious memory.

You disprove us quickly as do many others,
like a theory of formation, a series of magmatic processes
plus, weathering and erosion—an accumulation on the bones
of | fate | fallout | intrusion of igneous rock from below.

# PART III:

## And Beyond

## Goldilocks

From whither you come
to eat my porridge
out of this bowl
in my outstretch hand
and have restful dreams
on my bosomy bed.
I am the sweet spot—
nothing else survives
unless in-between.

## Boson

I'm supposed to be the
glue, but I can't stick
anymore (these days
I'm just weight)—
I am this mass that
fills life, yet I feel
microscopic—encom-
passing the same space
as everyone else, though
I wish to hold my own.
I am the composite
particle, the piece at
play that no one sees,
I'm behind the scenes
and often forgotten.
It is my fate to dis-
combobulate—to
expand but not fold,
to meld with the others
or remain the same—
spinning or not spinning
at a finite rate, and
maybe, just maybe,
changing the state
of the universe.

*Apotelesma*

When I look out at the expansive mass
of rock and fire before me,
I witness destruction in the arms of the one I love,
the uncertainty of crashing bodies
as a form of melancholia,
a sinister smile of destiny—the lodestone on the steel of fate—
an attempt to surmise expression of a lone figure
walking the road in lamplight, cloud cover
shadowing from above, nothing to
forecast an auspicious death by disillusionment.

My mother raised me to think of the stars
as distant angels and guardians
watching over me at night,
but all I see are lost
forms floating in the amniotic fluid of space,
beholding and mocking me,
then, in a blaze | smote | gone.

I rarely glance at the sky anymore,
though it is still bearing down on me
pushing me to and fro like the ocean
displaced by gravitational forces,
constant pressure against my limbs,
as I climb that final stretch
with the hope of being nearer to you.

Palms spread, I'm ever reaching out.
The darkness calls to me in dreams where I
see titans clash and farrowing fogs, mist
to blanket the clouds of my mind,
where language ceases, that is where I begin
and beyond that is you.

Once we thought we were the center of the universe
and sometimes still this thought pervades us, a
soft whispering of ego,
now it expands endlessly out around us, defining
us in spite of itself. This smallness incites
cosmic dreams within—
a minute fluttering, a wish to have wings
and as we dream we kill ourselves slowly
we falter as waking brings us closer to the edge
of the precipice,
between where knowledge and understanding meet,
where idealism and realism collide—
an endless spiral down through time,
meeting our inevitable fate, as written by the stars.

**Claire-Elise Baalke** is a life-long Alaskan. She grew up in rural Alaska and then a small town in Southwestern Alaska for the majority of her childhood. She started writing young—her first few projects were picture books. Later, when she began her Bachelor's degree in English at the University of Alaska Fairbanks, she started writing longer stories and novels. Her undergraduate honor's project was a fiction piece titled, *Of Many Kinds*. During her Master's degree in English she took creative writing workshops where she started writing more poetry.

More recently she started some Doctoral work as a Medieval Studies student at the University of New Mexico. Her research mainly focuses on the connections between women and dragons in Medieval literature, but she still writes fiction and poetry. She is particularly interested in ecocriticism, myth, and folklore which is likely the impetus for a lot of her poetic inspiration. She has poetry publications in *The Bangalore Review, Cirque Journal*, and the Flying Ketchup Press' collection titled, *Night Forest*.